Book One
Later Elementary

A DOZEN A DAY
SONGBOOK

ISBN 978-1-4234-7560-6

EXCLUSIVELY DISTRIBUTED BY

WILLIS MUSIC

HAL•LEONARD®

Visit Hal Leonard Online at
www.halleonard.com

Contact us:
Hal Leonard
7777 West Bluemound Road
Milwaukee, WI 53213
Email: info@halleonard.com

In Europe, contact:
Hal Leonard Europe Limited
42 Wigmore Street
Marylebone, London, W1U 2RN
Email: info@halleonardeurope.com

In Australia, contact:
Hal Leonard Australia Pty. Ltd.
4 Lentara Court
Cheltenham, Victoria, 3192 Australia
Email: info@halleonard.com.au

NOTE TO TEACHERS

This collection of Broadway, movie and pop hits can be used on its own or as supplementary material to the iconic *A Dozen A Day* technique series by Edna Mae Burnam. The pieces have been arranged to progress gradually, applying concepts and patterns from Burnam's technical exercises whenever possible. Suggested guidelines for use with the original series are also provided.

These arrangements are excellent supplements for any method and may also be used for sight-reading practice for more advanced students.

CONTENTS

Cabaret
from the Musical CABARET

Use with A Dozen A Day Book One,
after Group I (page 4).

Words by Fred Ebb
Music by John Kander
Arranged by Carolyn Miller

With energy and spunk (♩ = ca. 100)

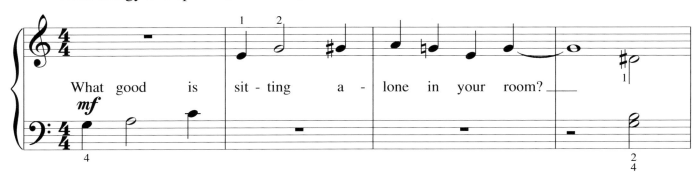

What good is sit - ting a - lone in your room?

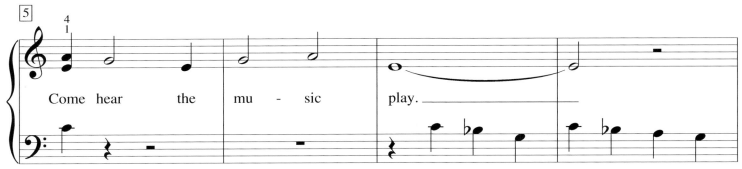

Come hear the mu - sic play.

Life is a cab - a - ret, old chum,

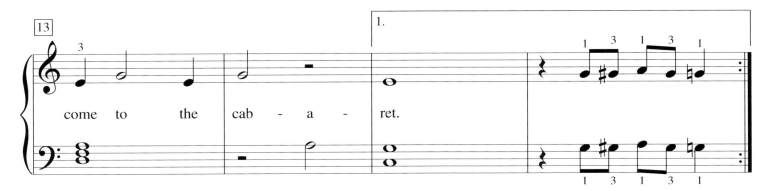

come to the cab - a - ret.

4

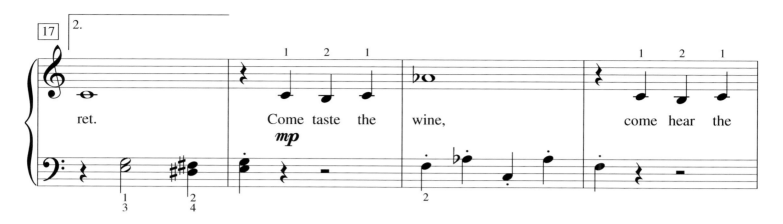

way. _____ _____ *cresc.* Life is a cab - a -

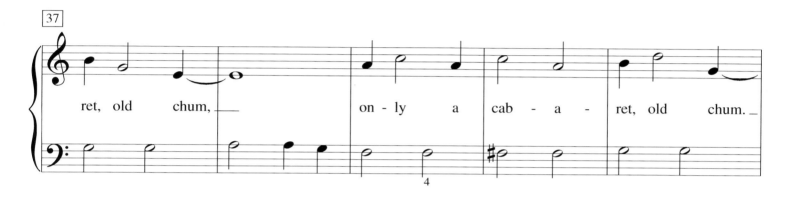

ret, old chum, _____ on - ly a cab - a - ret, old chum. _

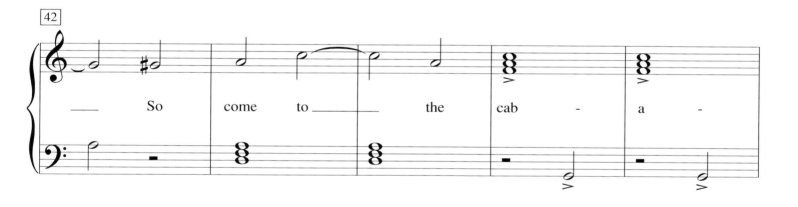

_____ So come to _____ the cab - a -

ret!

Zip-A-Dee-Doo-Dah

from Walt Disney's SONG OF THE SOUTH
from Disneyland and Walt Disney World's SPLASH MOUNTAIN

Use after Group I (page 4).

Words by Ray Gilbert
Music by Allie Wrubel
Arranged by Carolyn Miller

Zip - a-dee-doo - dah, zip - a-dee-ay!

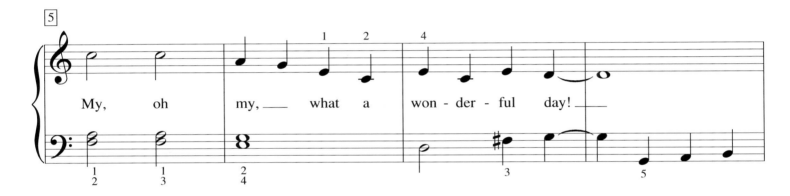

My, oh my, ___ what a won - der - ful day!

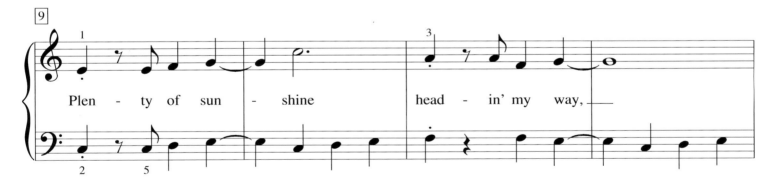

Plen - ty of sun - shine head - in' my way,

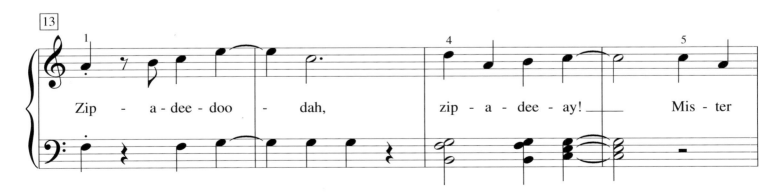

Zip - a-dee-doo - dah, zip - a-dee-ay! ___ Mis - ter

Blue - bird on my shoul - der, _____ it's the

legato

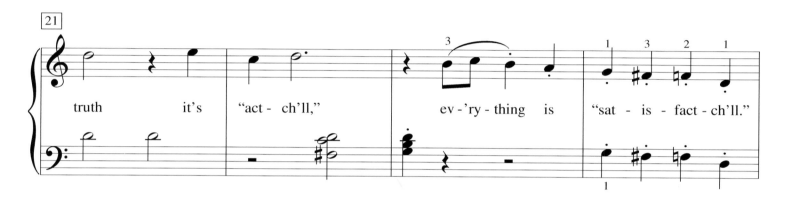

truth it's "act - ch'll," ev -'ry - thing is "sat - is - fact - ch'll."

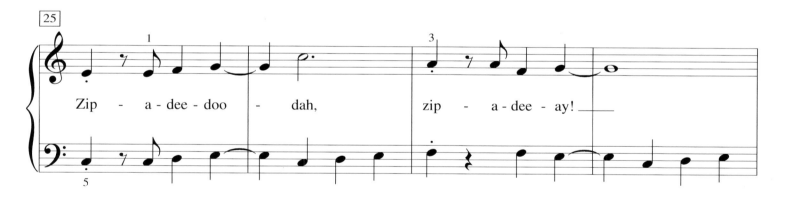

Zip - a - dee - doo - dah, zip - a - dee - ay! _____

Won - der - ful feel - ing, won - der - ful day.

Rock Around the Clock

Use after Group II (page 9).

Words and Music by Max C. Freedman
and Jimmy DeKnight
Arranged by Carolyn Miller

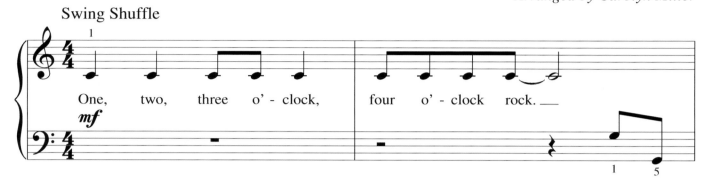

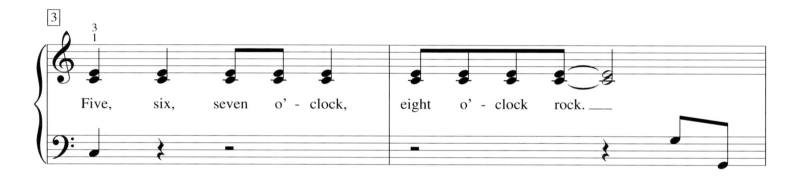

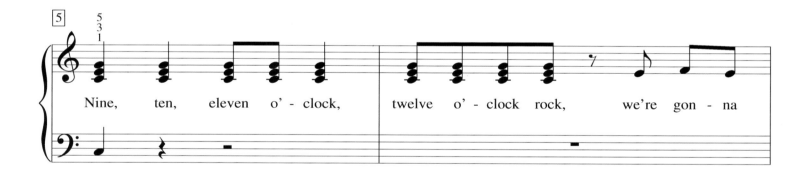

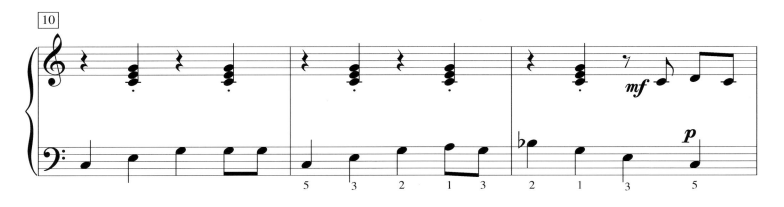

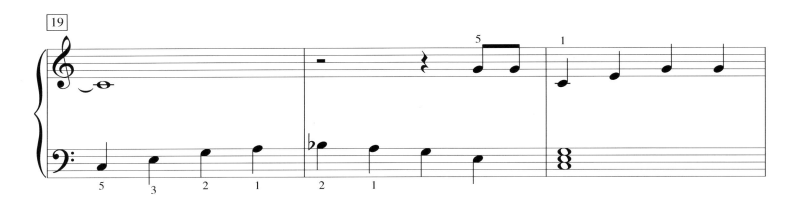

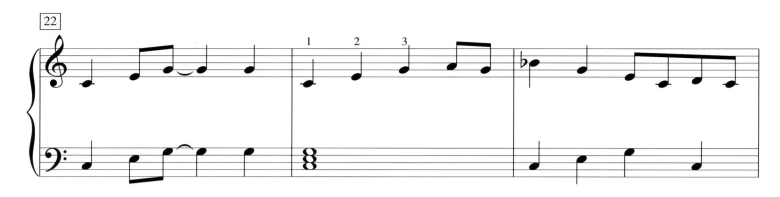

We're gon - na

rock a - round the clock to - night, __ we're gon - na rock, rock, rock, 'til

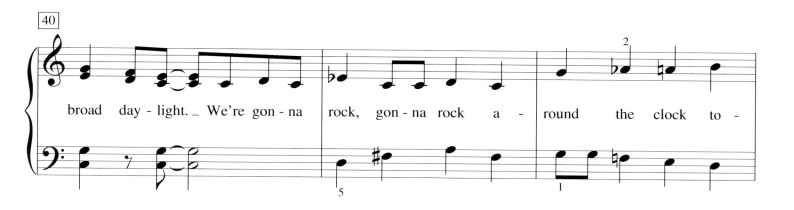

broad day - light. __ We're gon - na rock, gon - na rock a - round the clock to -

night.

p subito

Let It Be

Use after Group II (page 9).

Words and Music by John Lennon
and Paul McCartney
Arranged by Carolyn Miller

Moderately

When I find my-self in times of trou-ble, Moth-er Mar-y comes to me,

mp

speak-ing words of wis-dom, ___ let it be. _____ And

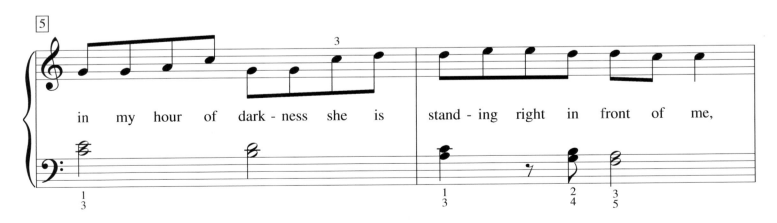

in my hour of dark-ness she is stand-ing right in front of me,

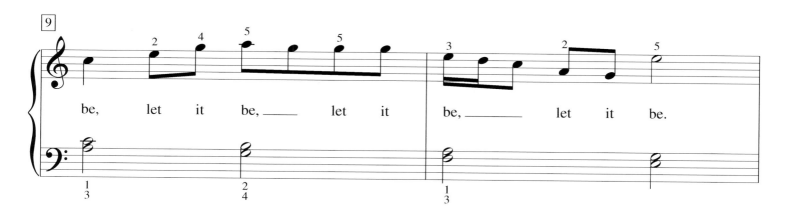

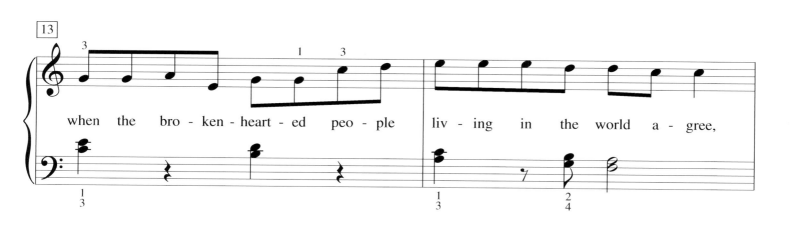

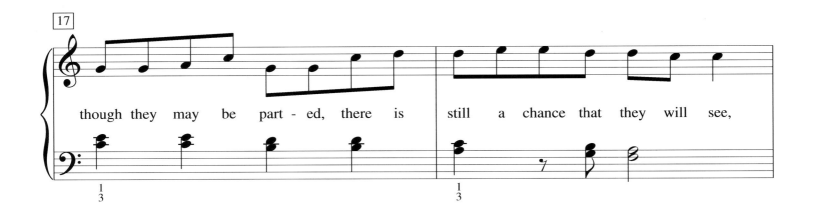

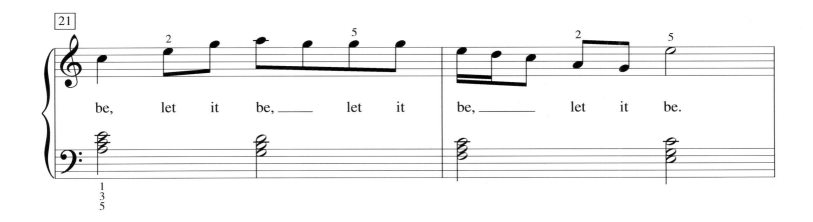

Whis - per words of wis - dom, let it be. _____ Let it

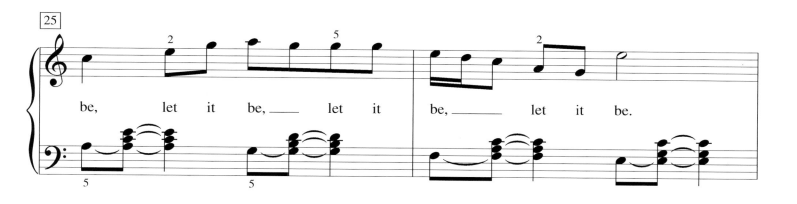

be, let it be, _____ let it be, _____ let it be.

Whis - per words of wis - dom, let it be. _____

f

p

rit.

The Wonderful Thing About Tiggers

from Walt Disney's THE MANY ADVENTURES OF WINNIE THE POOH

Use after Group III (page 14).

Words and Music by Richard M. Sherman
and Robert B. Sherman
Arranged by Carolyn Miller

Yo Ho
(A Pirate's Life for Me)
from PIRATES OF THE CARIBBEAN at Disneyland Park and Magic Kingdom Park

Use after Group III (page 14).

Words by Xavier Atencio
Music by George Bruns
Arranged by Carolyn Miller

If I Were a Rich Man

from the Musical FIDDLER ON THE ROOF

Use after Group IV (page 20).

Words by Sheldon Harnick
Music by Jerry Bock
Arranged by Carolyn Miller

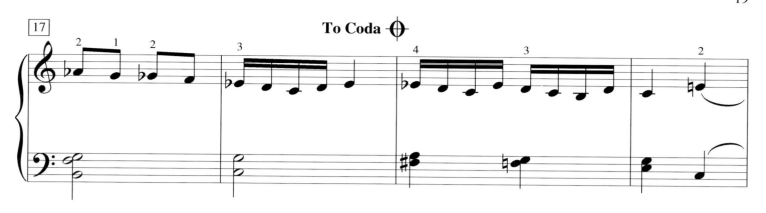

To Coda ⊕

mp *legato*

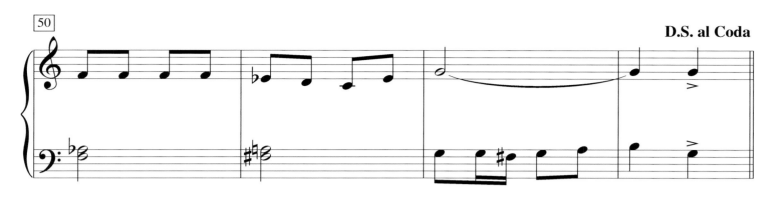

D.S. al Coda

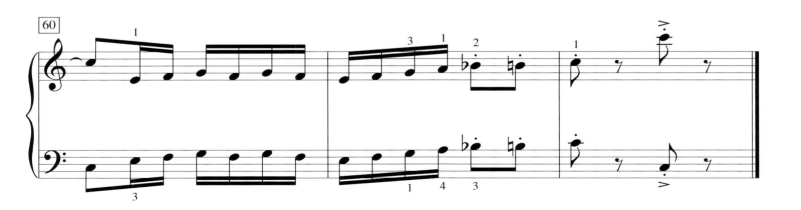

Give a Little Whistle

Use after Group IV (page 20).

Words by Ned Washington
Music by Leigh Harline

Cheerily

When you get in trou - ble and you don't know right from wrong, give a lit - tle
When you meet temp - ta - tion and the urge is ver - y strong, give a lit - tle

whis - tle! Give a lit - tle whis - tle!
whis - tle! Give a lit - tle

whis - tle!

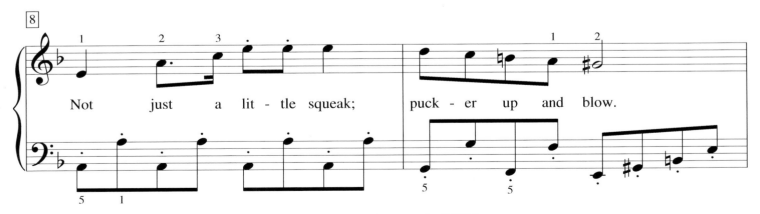

Not just a lit - tle squeak; puck - er up and blow.

And if your whis - tle's weak, yell, "Jim - i - ny Crick - et!"

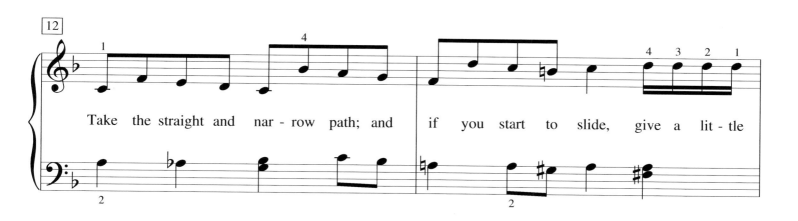

Take the straight and nar - row path; and if you start to slide, give a lit - tle

whis - tle! Give a lit - tle whis - tle! And

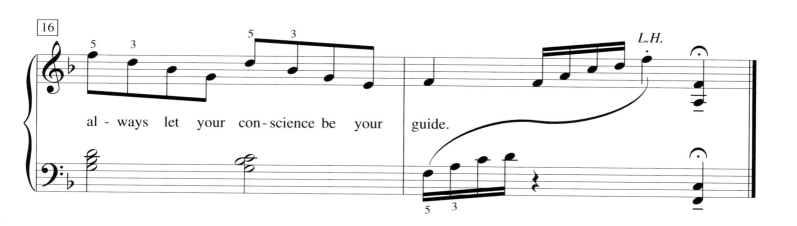

al - ways let your con - science be your guide.

Twist and Shout

Use after Group V (page 28).

Words and Music by Bert Russell
and Phil Medley
Arranged by Carolyn Miller

Moderate Rock beat

Well, work it on out, _____ you know you look so

good. _____ You know you got me go - in' now,

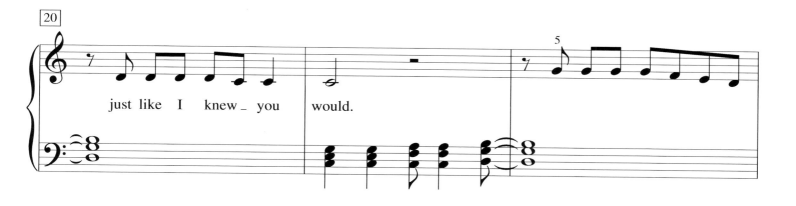

just like I knew _ you would.

come on and work it on out. Come on and work it on

out. ____ Well, work it on out, ____

you know you look so good. ___ You know you got me

go-in' now, just like I knew _ you would.

Climb Ev'ry Mountain

from THE SOUND OF MUSIC

Use after Group V (page 28).

Lyrics by Oscar Hammerstein II
Music by Richard Rodgers
Arranged by Carolyn Miller

Moderately, majestically

A DOZEN A DAY

by Edna Mae Burnam

The **A Dozen A Day** books are universally recognized as one of the most remarkable technique series on the market for all ages! Each book in this series contains short warm-up exercises to be played at the beginning of each practice session, providing excellent day-to-day training for the student. All book/audio versions include orchestrated accompaniments by Ric Ianonne.

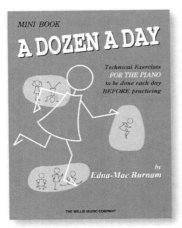

MINI BOOK
00404073 Book Only $5.99
00406472 Book/Audio $9.99

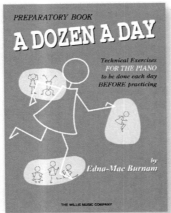

PREPARATORY BOOK
00414222 Book Only $5.99
00406476 Book/Audio $9.99

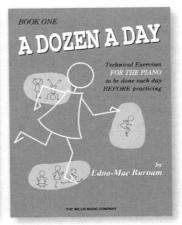

BOOK 1
00413366 Book Only $5.99
00406481 Book/Audio $9.99

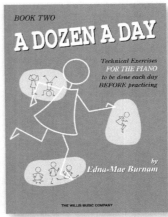

BOOK 2
00413826 Book Only $5.99
00406485 Book/Audio $9.99

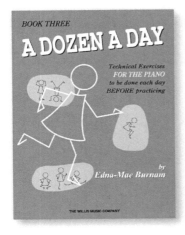

BOOK 3
00414136 Book Only $6.99
00416760 Book/Audio $10.99

BOOK 4
00415686 Book Only $6.99
00416761 Book/Audio $10.99

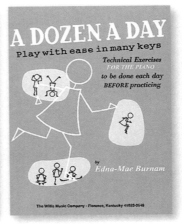

**PLAY WITH EASE
IN MANY KEYS**
00416395 Book Only $5.99

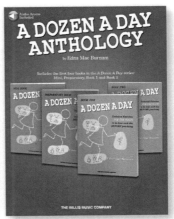

**A DOZEN A DAY
ANTHOLOGY**
00158307 Book/Audio $24.99

ALSO AVAILABLE:
The **A Dozen A Day Songbook** series containing Broadway, movie, and pop hits!

Visit Hal Leonard Online at **www.halleonard.com**

WILLIS MUSIC

EXCLUSIVELY DISTRIBUTED BY

HAL•LEONARD®

Prices, contents, and availability subject to change without notice. Prices listed in U.S. funds.